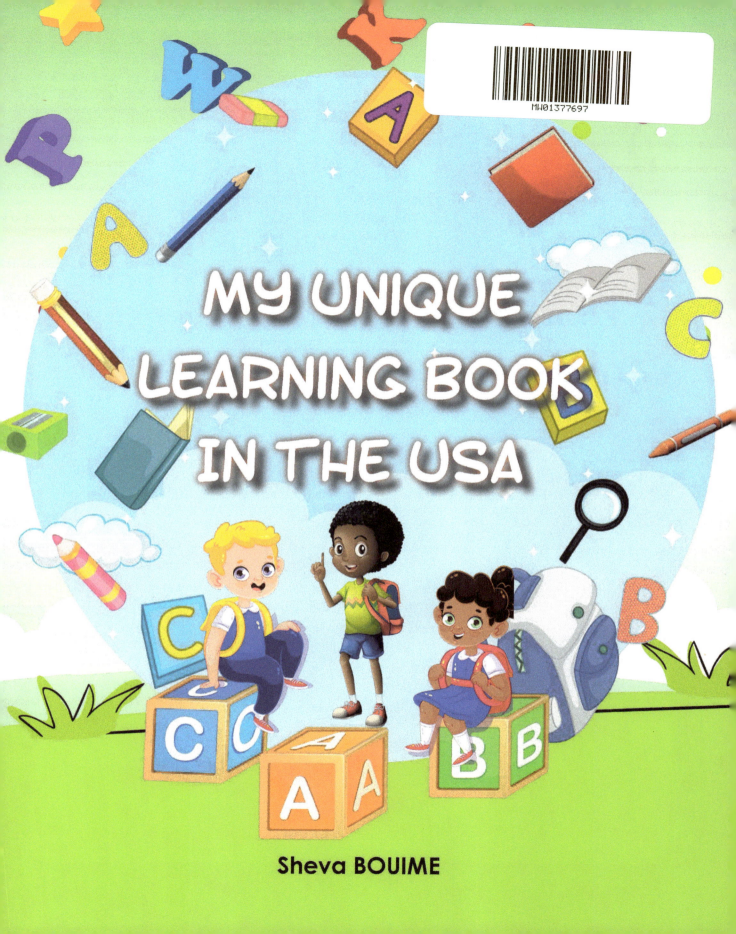

Copyright © 2024 Sheva Bouime
All rights reserved
First Edition

NEWMAN SPRINGS PUBLISHING
320 Broad Street
Red Bank, NJ 07701

First originally published by Newman Springs Publishing 2024

ISBN 979-8-89308-212-8 (Paperback)
ISBN 979-8-89308-213-5 (Digital)

Printed in the United States of America

Table of contents

P 4/32 — LEARNING ALPHABET

P 33/34 — MY BODY

P 35/46 — NUMBERS

P 47 — The days of the week

P 48/49 — The months of the year

P 50 — USA MAP

P 51 — Public Holidays

Alphabet

ALPHABETS

Aa Apple	Bb  Banana	Cc  Cake	Dd  Dolphin	Ee  Earth	Ff  Flower	Gg  Grapes
Hh  Hand	Ii  Ice-Cream	Jj  Jug	Kk  Kite	Ll  Lock	Mm  Mango	Nn  Nose
Oo  Orange	Pp  Pineapple	Qq ?  Question Mark	Rr  Rocket	Ss  Strawberry	Tt  Tree	Uu  Umbrella
	Vv  Van	Ww  Watermelon	Xx 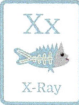 X-Ray	Yy  Yacht	Zz 0  Zero	

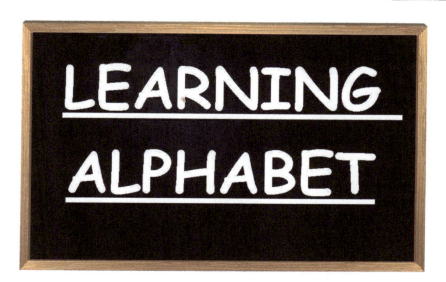

Alphabet

Alphabet

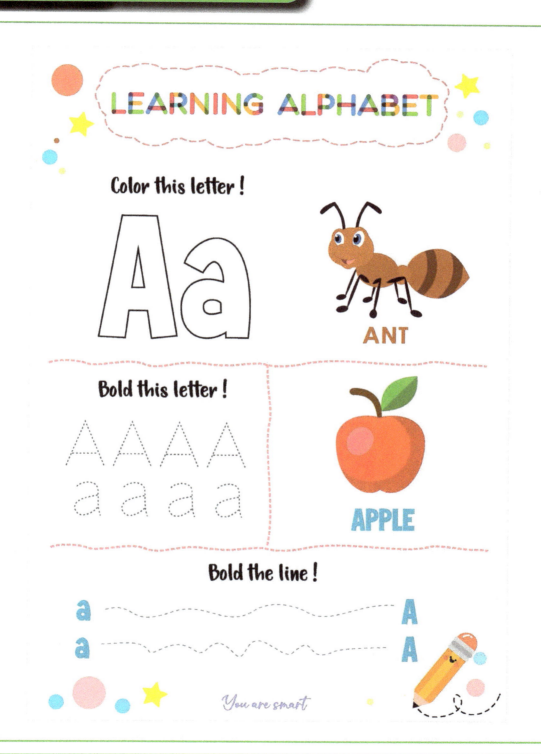

Alphabet

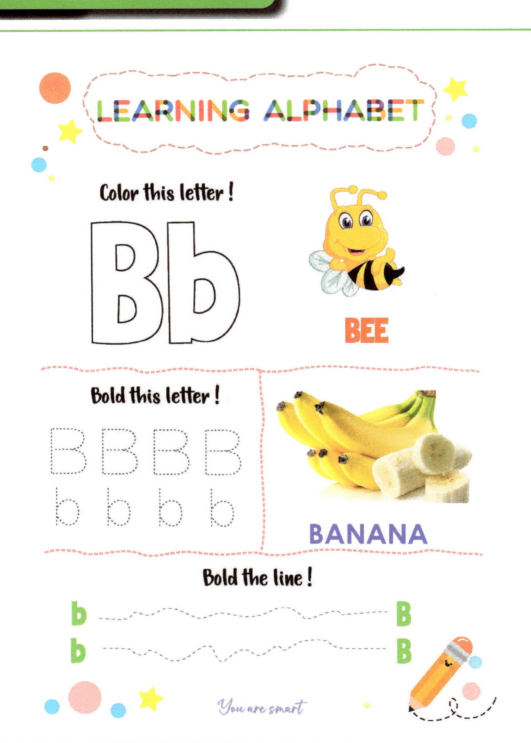

Alphabet

Alphabet

Alphabet

Alphabet

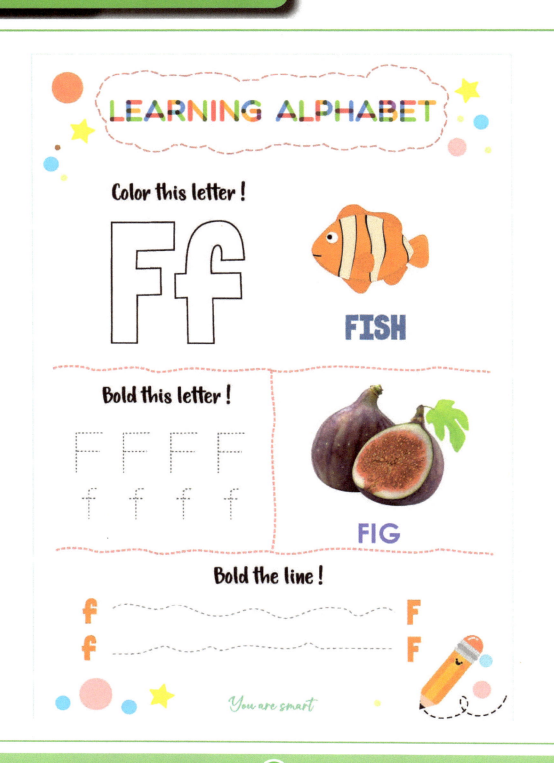

Alphabet

LEARNING ALPHABET

Color this letter !

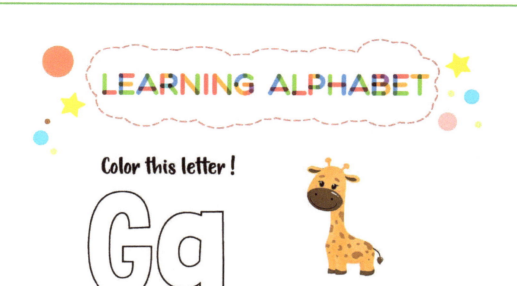

GIRAFFE

Bold this letter !

GRENADE

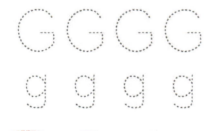

Bold the line !

You are smart

Alphabet

Alphabet

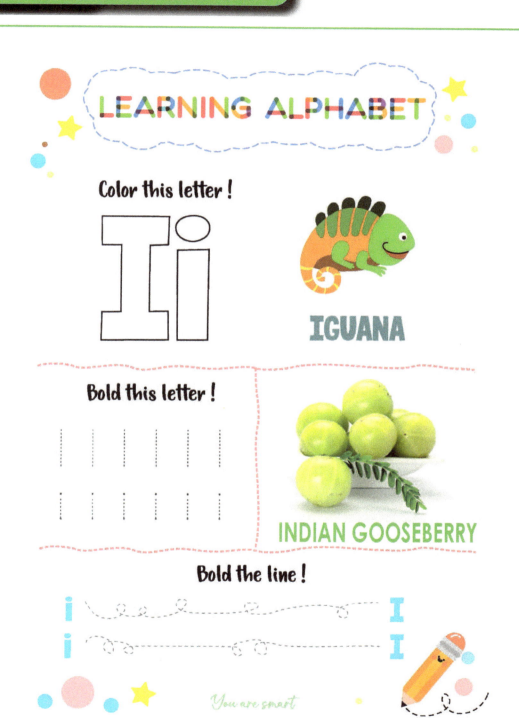

Alphabet

Alphabet

Color this letter !

KOALA

Bold this letter !

K K K K
k k k k

KIWI

Bold the line !

k   K
k   K

You are smart

Alphabet

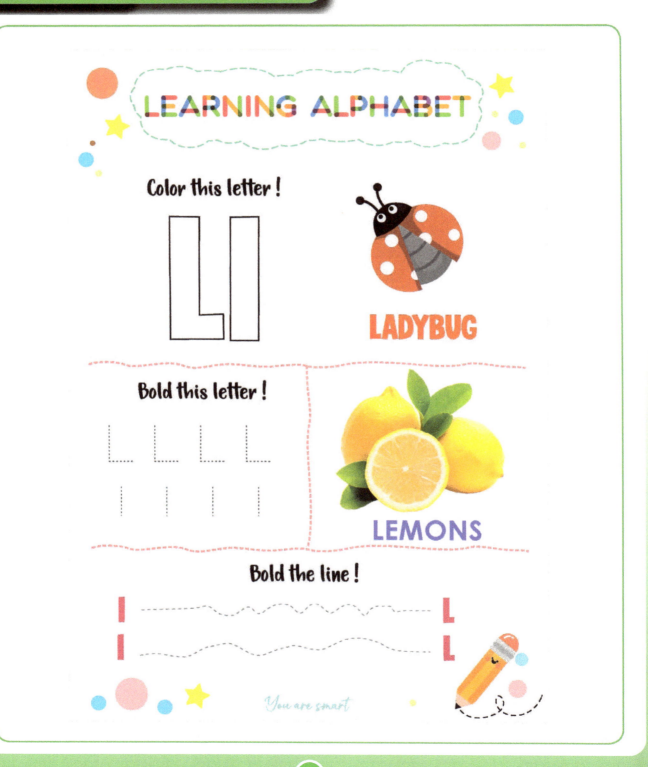

Alphabet

Alphabet

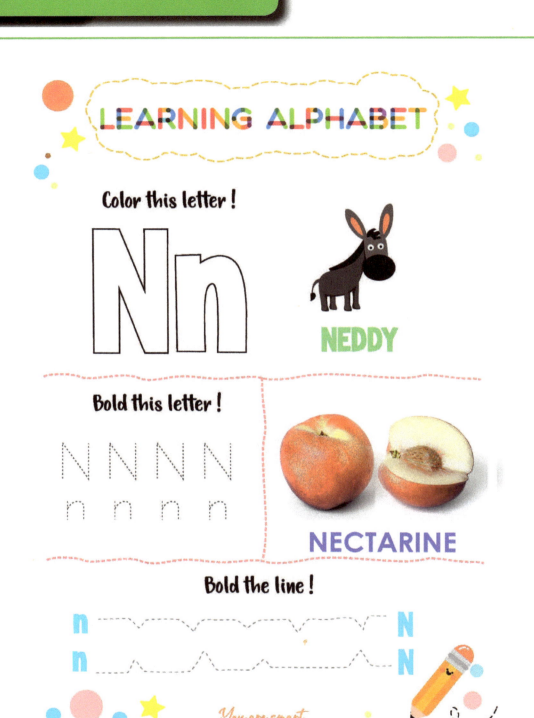

Alphabet

Alphabet

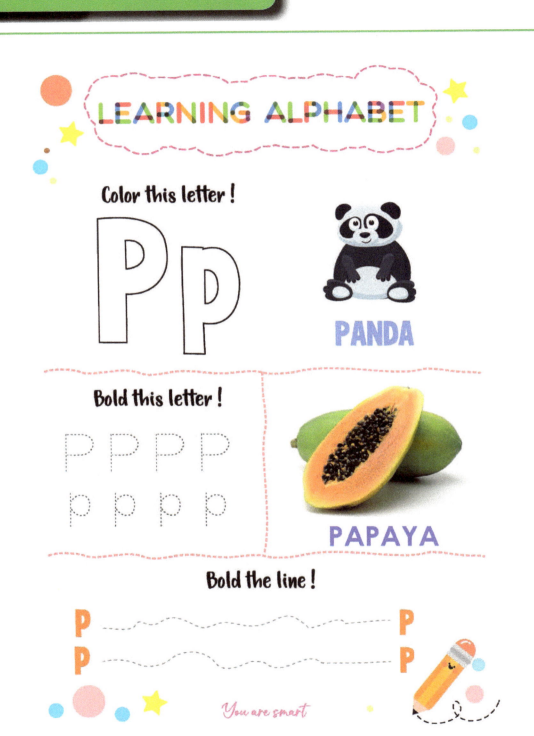

Alphabet

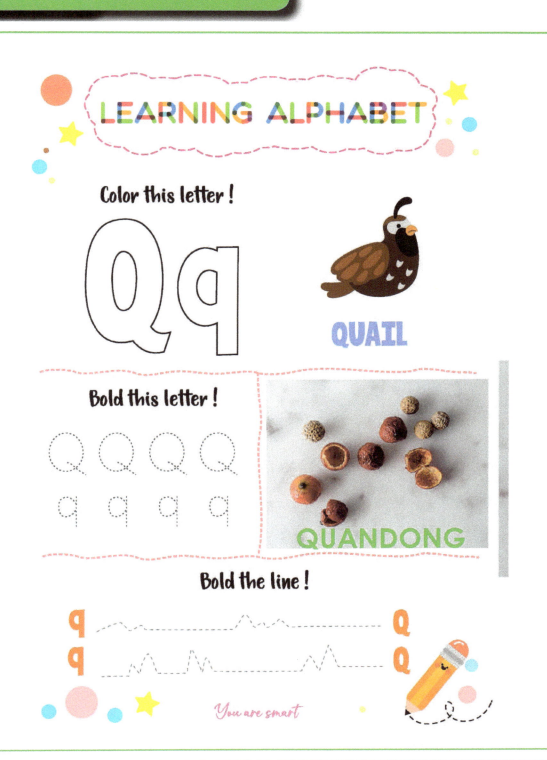

Alphabet

Alphabet

Color this letter!

Ss

SHARK

Bold this letter!

S S S S
s s s s

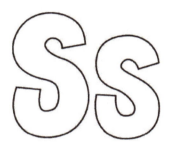

SAPADILLA

Bold the line!

S  S
S S

You are smart

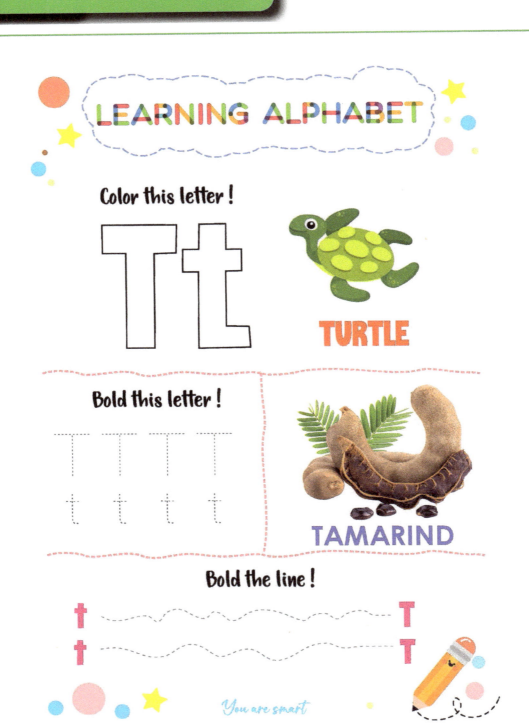

Alphabet

Alphabet

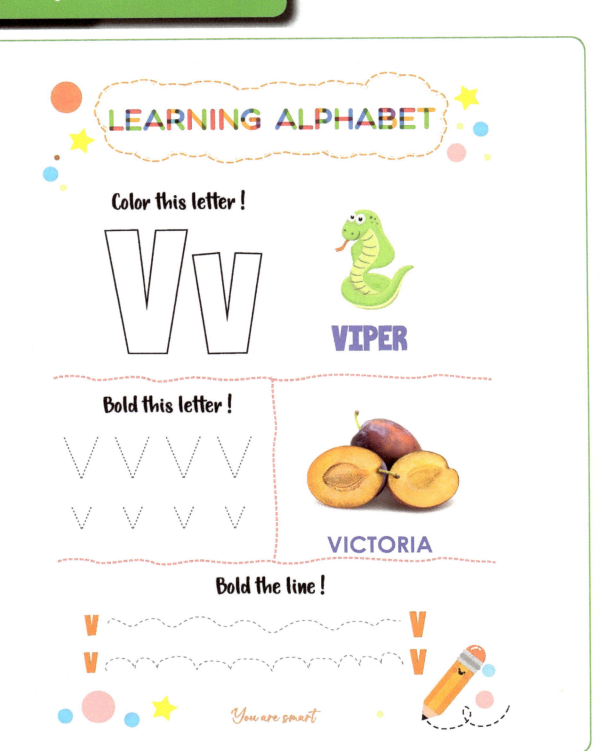

LEARNING ALPHABET

Color this letter !

Vv

VIPER

Bold this letter !

V V V V
v v v v

VICTORIA

Bold the line !

You are smart

Alphabet

Color this letter !

WHALE

Bold this letter !

Watermelon

Bold the line !

  You are smart

Alphabet

Color this letter !

X-RAY FISH

Bold this letter !

xylophone

Bold the line !

You are smart

Alphabet

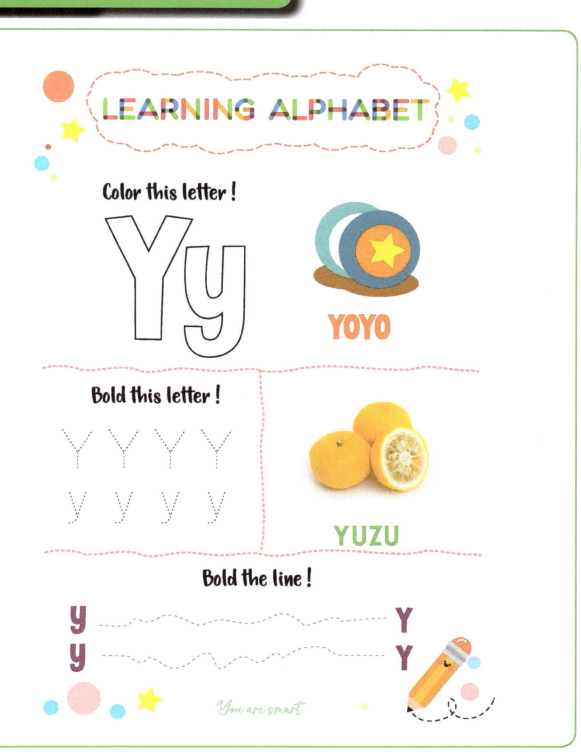

Alphabet

Color this letter!

ZEBRA

Bold this letter!

Z Z Z Z
Z Z Z Z

ZANTE

Bold the line!

You are smart

MY BODY

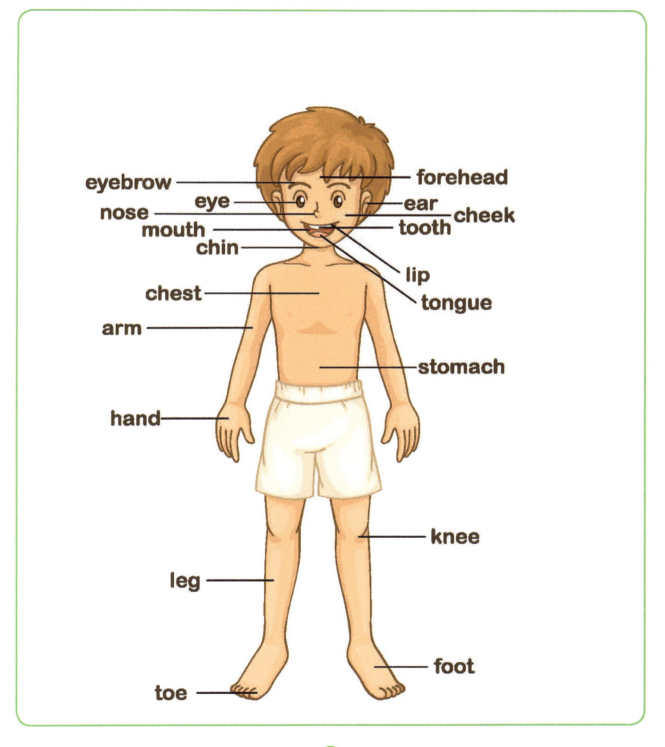

MY BODY

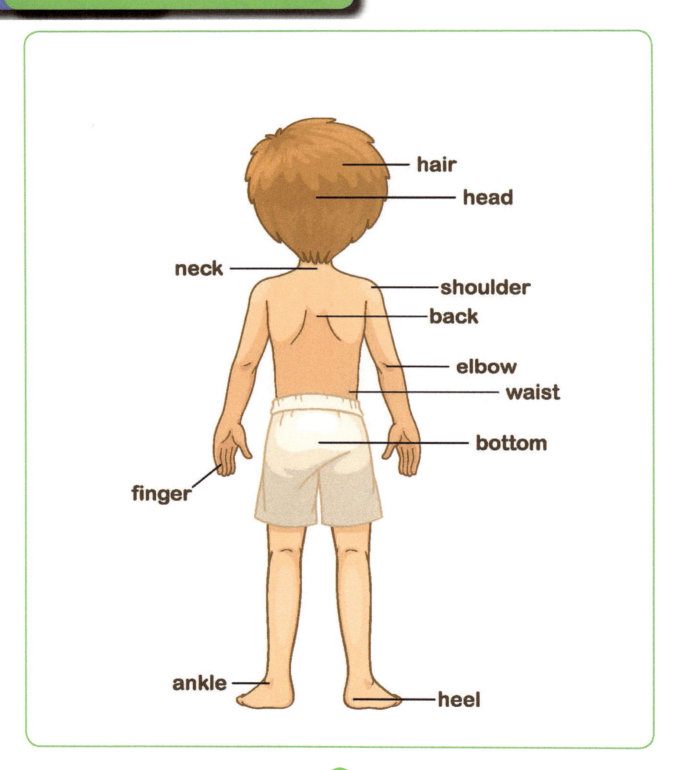

NUMBERS

Count
1 to 10

NUMBERS

Count

NUMBERS

NUMBERS

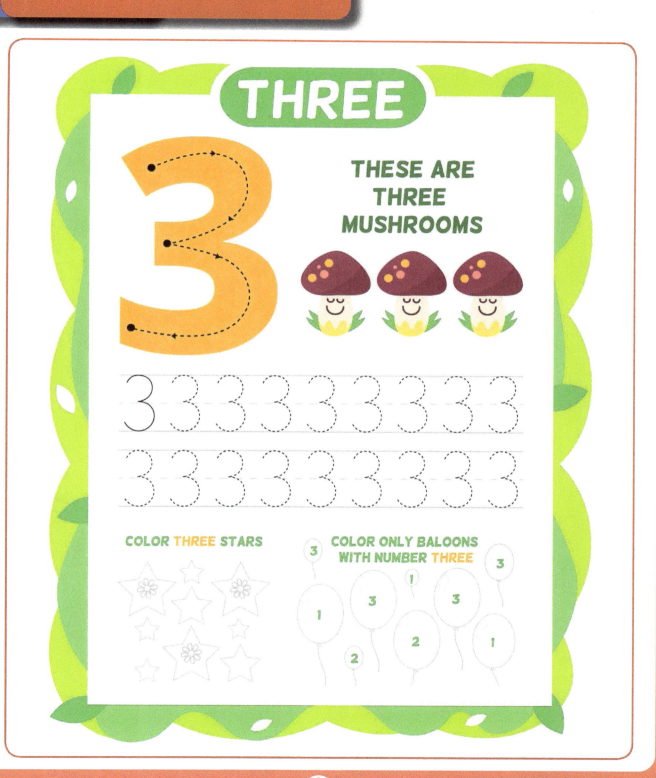

NUMBERS

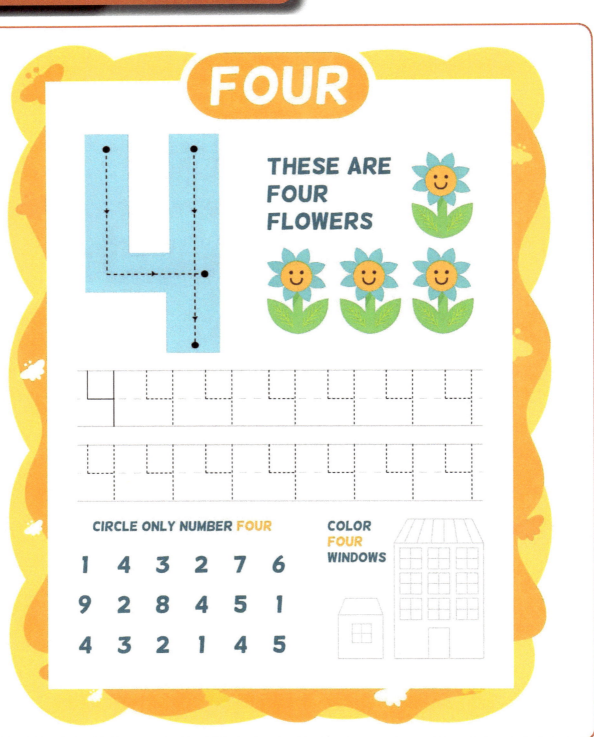

NUMBERS

NUMBERS

NUMBERS

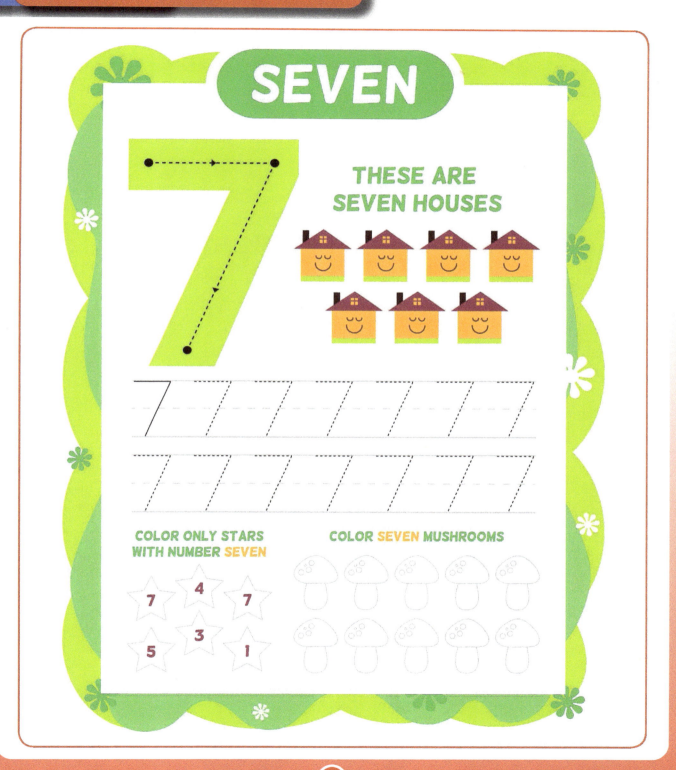

NUMBERS

EIGHT

THESE ARE EIGHT APPLES

FIND AND CIRCLE ALL NUMBERS EIGHT

COLOR EIGHT FLOWER

NUMBERS

NUMBERS

10

YOU HAVE TEN FINGERS ON YOUR HANDS

COLOR TEN BUTTERFLIES

CIRCLE ONLY NUMBER TEN

10 4 3 2 7
9   2 8 10 5
6   3 10 1 4
8   4 9 2 10

The days of the week

MONTHS

THE MONTHS OF THE YEAR

MONTHS

THE MONTHS OF THE YEAR

USA MAP

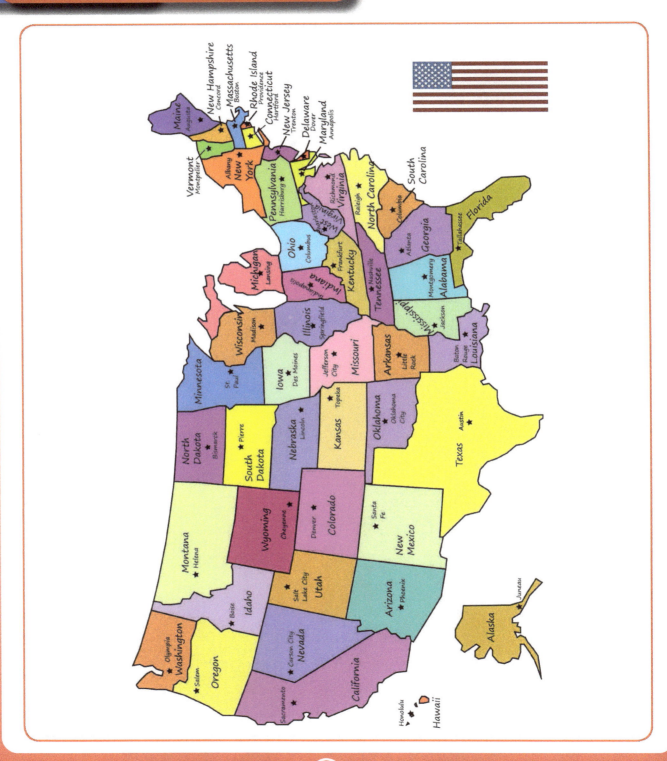

Public Holidays

▶ **Martin Luther King's**, who celebrates the birth of Martin Luther King Jr., a great defender of the black and wider ethnic minority community of the United States of America, and is celebrated on the 3rd Monday in January.

▶ **President's Day**, celebrated on the 3rd Monday in February, which was instituted to pay tribute to George Washington, the first US president, and then gradually became an opportunity to also celebrate Abraham Lincoln, the hero president of the Civil War.

▶ **Columbus's Day**, which celebrates the famous pioneer who discovered America every second Monday in October.

▶ **New Year's Day**, January 1, is also a holiday in the US. For a century, it has been starting with the Times Square Ball (a kind of huge crystal ball) that descends from the top of the building at 11:59 p.m. to touch the ground at midnight.

▶ **Memorial Day**, the last Monday in May, is celebrated in memory of American veterans who lost their lives in conflict and war.

▶ **Independence Day**, every July 4, is the American National Day that celebrates the anniversary of the Declaration of Independence signed on July 4, 1776.

▶ **Labor Day**, Labour Day, takes place on the 1st Monday of September. It celebrates the working-class force that helps to create the country's prosperity.

▶ **Veterans Day**, November 11, is a commemorative day seen in tribute to the fighters of the First World War.

▶ **Thanksgiving** celebrates the anniversary of the first harvest obtained by American settlers from England. This date has become a day of thanksgiving to thank God for all the happiness received during the year. Celebrated on Thursday of November and today secular, Thanksgiving is certainly the most popular festival in the United States.

▶ **Christmas**, which is the only unused religious holiday in the United States, on December 25.

The Star-Spangled Banner

O say can you see, by the dawn's early light,
What so proudly we hailed at the twilight's last gleaming,
Whose broad stripes and bright stars through the perilous fight,
O'er the ramparts we watched, were so gallantly streaming?
And the rocket's red glare, the bombs bursting in air,
Gave proof through the night that our flag was still there;
O say does that star-spangled banner yet wave
O'er the land of the free and the home of the brave?

On the shore dimly seen through the mists of the deep,
Where the foe's haughty host in dread silence reposes,
What is that which the breeze, o'er the towering steep,
As it fitfully blows, half conceals, half discloses?
Now it catches the gleam of the morning's first beam,
In full glory reflected now shines in the stream:
'Tis the star-spangled banner, O long may it wave
O'er the land of the free and the home of the brave.

And where is that band who so vauntingly swore
That the havoc of war and the battle's confusion,
A home and a country, should leave us no more?
Their blood has washed out their soul footsteps' pollution.
No refuge could save the hireling and slave
From the terror of flight, or the gloom of the grave:
And the star-spangled banner in triumph doth wave,
O'er the land of the free and the home of the brave.

O thus be it ever, when freemen shall stand
Between their loved homes and the war's desolation.
Blest with vict'ry and peace, may the Heav'n rescued land
Praise the Power that hath made and preserved us a nation!
Then conquer we must, when our cause it is just,
And this be our motto: "In God is our trust."
And the star-spangled banner in triumph shall wave
O'er the land of the free and the home of the brave!

Printed in the USA
CPSIA information can be obtained
at www.ICGtesting.com
LVHW071939270924
792310LV00011B/106